follow me

Making Art

CAROLINE GRIMSHAW

World Book

in association with TWOCAN

j701 GRI

follow me *and find out (almost) everything about making art!*

follow me

Making Art

CREATIVE AND EDITORIAL DIRECTOR
CONCEPT/FORMAT/DESIGN/TEXT
CAROLINE GRIMSHAW

TEXT EDITOR
IQBAL HUSSAIN

ART CONSULTANT
JULIA WEINER COURTAULD INSTITUTE, LONDON

ILLUSTRATIONS
NICK DUFFY ◊ SPIKE GERRELL
CAROLINE GRIMSHAW

THANKS TO
LAURA CARTWRIGHT PICTURE RESEARCH
BRONWEN LEWIS EDITORIAL SUPPORT
MELISSA TUCKER U.S. EDITOR

TITLES IN THIS SERIES
◊ YOU AND ME ◊ OUR WORLD
◊ OUR HOMES ◊ MAKING ART

CONCEIVED AND DESIGNED BY CAROLINE GRIMSHAW FOR
TWO-CAN PUBLISHING LTD, 346 OLD STREET, LONDON EC1V 9NQ

COPYRIGHT © CAROLINE GRIMSHAW/TWO-CAN PUBLISHING LTD, 1998.

FOR INFORMATION ON OTHER WORLD BOOK PRODUCTS,
CALL 1-800-255-1750, EXT. 2238, OR VISIT US AT OUR WEB SITE AT
HTTP://WWW.WORLDBOOK.COM

FIRST PUBLISHED IN THE UNITED STATES AND CANADA BY
WORLD BOOK INC., 525 W. MONROE, CHICAGO, IL 60661
IN ASSOCIATION WITH TWO-CAN PUBLISHING LTD.

LIBRARY OF CONGRESS CATALOGING-IN-PUBLICATION DATA
GRIMSHAW, CAROLINE.
    MAKING ART/CAROLINE GRIMSHAW; TEXT EDITOR IQBAL HUSSAIN.
    P. CM. — (FOLLOW ME)
    INCLUDES INDEX.
    SUMMARY: DISCUSSES ART HISTORY, VARIOUS STYLES OF ART, THE
MOTIVES FOR MAKING ART, AND HOW ART RELATES TO PEOPLE AND
NATURE.
    ISBN 0-7166-8804-2 (HC). — ISBN 0-7166-8805-0 (SC).
    1. ART—JUVENILE LITERATURE. [1. ART.] I. HUSSAIN, IQBAL, 1971- .
II. SERIES: FOLLOW ME (CHICAGO, ILL.)
N7440.G75 1998   97-38113
701—DC21

PRINTED IN SPAIN
1 2 3 4 5 6 7 8 9 10 01 00 99 98 97

Welcome to a special book all about Making Art

Meet your guides...

Hop

Take a giant hop with this bunny to Show Me panels. These activities will help you to see for yourself that the facts you are reading are true. Look out for this hot spot:

 show me

Skip

Skip along to Tricky Test Time panels with this kangaroo. Here you will find puzzles, quizzes, and activities. The answers are on the last page of the book. Watch out for this hot spot:

 tricky test time

Jump

Take a looping leap with this flying fish. The Follow Me panels let you choose to move to a page further on in the book. This clever little fish will point out the links between art, the people who make it, and the world. Follow the fish when you see this hot spot:

 follow me

Look out for all sorts of things hiding on the pages when you see this hot spot:

Find it!

You're just a Hop, Skip, and Jump away from knowing (almost) everything about making art!

Where should you start? Just choose a subject and turn to that page.

Take your pick and let's get going.
f◎ll◎w me

Painting, drawing, sculpture, and so much more...

It's all **art**

Some people use their imagination and skill to create something for themselves or for others to share. We call what they produce "art." People who make art are called artists.

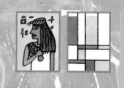

Find it!

There are five tiny pieces of art on these pages. Find them!

Different kinds of art

Art may be something that you can see, such as a painting, drawing, photograph, or sculpture. This is called visual art. Art may also be something that you can hear, such as music, or something that you can read, such as a poem or a story. In this book, we will look at visual art.

tricky test time

One of these is not art – which one?

A

B

C

follow me

Some artists have used the human body as a paintbrush. Follow me to page 11.

① Painting

A painting is made by spreading paint onto a surface, such as paper, wood, or thick cloth called canvas. The artist puts the paint on using a tool. This could be a brush, a knife – even the artist's fingers!

② Drawing

A drawing is a picture made with materials such as chalks, crayons, pencils, or inks. Most drawings are made on paper. Artists often make rough drawings, or sketches, to jot down their ideas and the things they see.

Many different shapes and sizes

◊ Some artists have grand ideas. They may use unusual materials to show us how they feel about the world. Between 1980 and 1983, the artists Christo and Jeanne-Claude created a work of art called *Surrounded Islands*. This involved covering in pink fabric the water around 11 islands in Biscayne Bay in Florida.

◊ A miniature is a small painting, usually of a person. It may be no bigger than a fingernail!

 show me

Paint a miniature of a friend, on a piece of paper the size of a postage stamp. What is the smallest miniature you are able to paint?

---

③ Photograph

A photograph is art when it shows us a new way of looking at a scene or a situation.

The Italian artist Leonardo da Vinci (1452-1519) made hundreds of sketches in his notebooks.

---

④ Sculpture

A sculpture is a solid piece of art made out of wood, metal, clay, stone, or other materials. It may be free-standing, which means that you can walk around it. Other sculpture may be in relief, which means that it either bulges out of a flat surface or is cut into the surface.

◊ FREE-STANDING   ◊ RELIEF

This free-standing sculpture, called *The Kiss*, was carved from marble between 1901 and 1904 by the French sculptor Auguste Rodin (1840-1917).

---

⑤ Other types of art

◊ In parts of Africa, people paint brightly colored patterns and pictures on their bodies.
◊ In Southeast Asia, craftsmen make beautiful jewelry using gold and precious stones.
◊ The ancient Greeks made pottery decorated with curved designs and pictures of animals.

Artists make sculptures from many different materials. Follow me to page 12.

Making art

for many different reasons...

Let's take a look at the first art ever made and some of the reasons people have continued producing art ever since.

The first art

The oldest known examples of art date from about 30,000 years ago. This was during the Old Stone Age.

◊ SCULPTURE

Prehistoric artists carved sculptures of animals and people in bone, ivory (from animal tusks), or stone.

◊ PAINTING

Prehistoric artists used three main colors: black, red, and yellow. They made them from soil, rocks, grass, roots, and berries. They applied the paint with their fingers, or with brushes made of twigs, feathers, or fur. They also blew paint through tubes made of bone.

follow me

Some artists are never taught how to paint. Follow me to page 16.

show me

Make your own prehistoric paintings, using natural colors. Ask an adult to add hot water to coffee (brown), onion skins (yellow), beetroot (red), and spinach (green). Once the colored water has cooled, you can use it as paint.

Most prehistoric paintings are of large animals, such as cattle, deer, and horses. They may have been made to bring people luck while hunting. The painting shown above was discovered in a cave in France. It is about 20,000 years old.

Some reasons why people make art

1 EXPLORING THE WORLD

Artists try to find new ways of looking at familiar scenes and objects.

In 1921, the French painter Fernand Léger (1881-1955) used simple blocks of flat color to paint this picture of a table.

2 SHARING BELIEFS

People have made art about their beliefs and gods for thousands of years. Some artists show scenes from the Christian holy book, the Bible. Buddhist artists make statues and paintings of their leader, Buddha.

3 EARNING A LIVING

Many artists make art so that they can sell their work and earn money. Some artists have patrons, who pay the artists to produce work for them.

4 SHARING FEELINGS

The Norwegian artist Edvard Munch (1863-1944) painted many pictures about feelings such as fear and loneliness.

The Scream was painted in 1893.

5 RECORDING EVENTS

Before the invention of the camera, the only way to record images of what was happening in the world was by drawing, painting, or sculpting them.

This painting was made in the 1450's by the Italian artist Paolo Uccello (1397-1475). It shows the Battle of San Romano.

tricky test time

Follow the twisty routes to match each work of art to the religion that inspired the artist to make it.

ISLAM

SHINTOISM

HINDUISM

CHRISTIANITY

6 BRINGING MANY PEOPLE TOGETHER

In 1991, 10,000 people made the world's longest sand sculpture. It was built at Myrtle Beach, South Carolina, and was almost 87,054 feet (26,380 meters) long.

follow me

Looking at art can tell us about the history of the world. Follow me to page 22.

Let's look at

Choosing a **subject**

People make art about what is important to them. Some subjects have always been popular with artists. They include nature and the land, people, animals, events, and feelings.

WHAT DO WE MEAN BY SUBJECT?

The subject of a work of art is what it is about. It may be a bowl of fruit, a bird in flight, or a person's face. Other subjects are things that you cannot see or touch, such as feelings, moods, and ideas.

 tricky test time

To find a square on this grid, use the numbers down the side and the colors along the top. One square is labeled to help you. In which square is the flower? What subjects are in these squares: 4-red, 2-blue, 3-green?

1	🚢	🍍	🦉	✈️
2	THIS SQUARE IS 2 -RED	🌼	🎻	🏘️
3	🐎	👤	🌊	🪐
4	🌲	🚐	🏺	🐦

① Nature and the land

Beautiful, brightly colored pictures of the countryside were painted in India and Persia (now Iran) between the 1500's and 1700's. They appeared in books of religious stories.

 follow me

Find out more about making art about our planet. Follow me to page 20.

② People and portraits

A piece of art is called a portrait when its subject is a person, or a group of people. Artists have created portraits of gods, kings and queens, rulers, film stars, musicians, and ordinary people.

 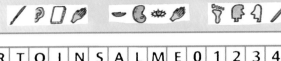 **tricky test time**

Leonardo da Vinci made a very famous portrait. Use the key to find out what it is called and when it was painted.

R	T	O	I	N	S	A	L	M	E	0	1	2	3	4	5

 **follow me**

How do artists make the human body the subject of their art? Follow me to page 18.

Find it!

There are six tiny paintings on these pages: three portraits, two animal pictures, and one abstract picture. Find them!

③ Events
(THINGS THAT HAPPEN)

Artists may capture dramatic events, such as wars, or they may record more peaceful scenes. This painting is by the French artist Georges Seurat (1859-1891). It is called *Bathers at Asnières* and shows what it was like to go swimming in the late 1800's.

④ Animals in art

A mosaic is a work of art made of small pieces of colored stone or glass. This mosaic of a snake was made about 500 years ago, by the Aztec people of Mexico.

⑤ Abstract art

Artists may use colors, patterns, and shapes to represent feelings and ideas. They may decide not to show images of recognizable objects and scenes. This is called abstract art.

 show me

Make your own animal mosaic. Draw an animal shape on a sheet of paper. Then stick small, square pieces of colored paper on it. You could also use shells, pebbles, and dried beans.

9

One of the oldest ways of making art is

Painting

Since prehistoric times, artists have covered surfaces in paint to show what they are thinking and feeling. Paintings give us enjoyment and change the way we see the world.

Find it!

Find three palettes and four tiny tubes of paint on these pages.

What is paint?

Paint is made by mixing powdered colors, called pigments, with sticky liquids, called binders. Early artists made pigments from stones, earth, berries, roots, and burned wood.

USING DIFFERENT TYPES OF PAINT	
WATERCOLOR PAINT	MIXED WITH WATER
OIL PAINT	MIXED WITH OIL
TEMPERA PAINT	MIXED WITH EGG YOLK

tricky test time

Make your way through this true (**T**) or false (**F**) maze to learn more about pigments.

Cochineal (bright red) is made from rose petals.

Burnt sienna (red-brown) is made from burned wood.

START HERE

Ultramarine (bright blue) was once made from a rare stone called lapis lazuli.

The ancient Greeks and Romans made Tyrian purple (blue-red) from crushed shellfish.

THE END

follow me

Artists use paint in all kinds of ways. Follow me to page 11.

Looking at color

USING COLOR

Artists use colors to help them to tell stories. They may use certain colors to express moods or feelings.

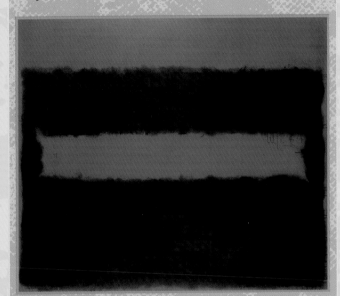

The American artist Mark Rothko (1903-1970) painted *Black on Maroon* between 1958 and 1959. He wanted to see the effects that different colors had on people looking at his work.

MIXING COLORS TOGETHER

In painting, red, yellow, and blue are called primary colors. You can mix them together to make any other color, except white. Two primary colors mixed together make secondary colors.

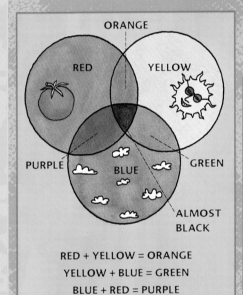

RED + YELLOW = ORANGE
YELLOW + BLUE = GREEN
BLUE + RED = PURPLE
RED + YELLOW + BLUE = ALMOST BLACK

show me

Experiment with colors by mixing together red, yellow, and blue paint. What colors do you make when you mix together two secondary colors? Do colors seem to change when you put different colors next to them?

Painting with oils

Oil paint dries slowly, so an artist can change a painting many times while the paint is wet. Oil paint can be applied to a canvas in many layers. It may be used straight from the tube, or it may be made thinner by adding a clear liquid, called turpentine.

follow me

Artists have found other ways of using their faces and bodies in their work. Follow me to page 19.

Painting without a brush

The American artist Jackson Pollock (1912-1956) nailed his canvases to the floor and dripped, splashed, or poured the paint on to them. He was called an "action painter."

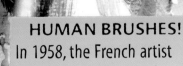

HUMAN BRUSHES!

In 1958, the French artist Yves Klein (1928-1962) asked his models to cover their bodies with blue paint and roll around on canvases!

11

Looking at art that is
Not flat!

Art can be anything at all, as long as it is made with imagination and skill. Some artists make models, others set up artistic events.

Find it!
There are two tiny masks, three marble statues, and two bricks on these pages. Find them!

Making sculpture

A sculpture is a solid, or three-dimensional, work of art. The earliest known examples of sculpture were made between 27,000 and 32,000 years ago.

1 GODS AND PHARAOHS

In ancient Egypt, sculptors carved large, stone statues of gods and pharaohs. Temples were decorated with carvings showing important events, such as festivals and victories.

follow me
People are sometimes inspired by the art of ancient cultures. Follow me to page 14.

2 MARBLE STATUES

About 2,500 years ago, ancient Greek sculptors made lifelike statues from white marble. They carved many standing figures of young men and women.

3 AFRICAN SCULPTURE

Traditional African sculpture includes carvings, masks, and statues. Artists model faces with exaggerated features to show different feelings, such as fear or respect.

① Collage

A collage is a piece of art made by sticking materials or objects onto a surface.

This collage is called *Opened by Customs*. It was created by the German artist Kurt Schwitters (1887-1948) between 1937 and 1938. It is made up of wrapping paper, stamps, and torn pieces of newspaper.

show me

Make a collage from natural materials: seeds, leaves, flowers, grass, feathers, sand, pebbles, and shells. Arrange them on a sheet of paper and glue them down.

tricky test time

There are five pieces missing from this sculpture. Find the pieces to complete it.

A B C D E F G H

② "Found objects"

Some artists use everyday objects, such as furniture or machines, in new and exciting ways. We call the objects that they select "found objects."

This sculpture was made in 1981 by the English artist Bill Woodrow. It is pieced together from a washing machine, an ironing board, and a car door.

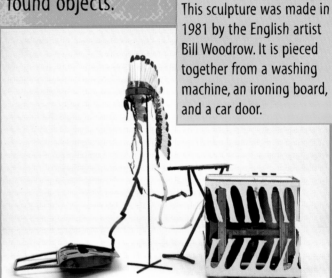

◊ In 1976, the American artist Carl Andre made a sculpture by stacking 120 bricks in two layers to form a rectangle. Some people found it interesting, but others could not understand why it was art. What do you think?

Art can be an event

An event may be art if it is designed to affect how people think, feel, or behave. In 1958, Yves Klein showed a work called *Le Vide* (meaning emptiness, in French). It was made up of a bare gallery (a place where art is shown) that was painted white inside and blue outside.

follow me

Follow me to page 19 to read about an artist who makes extremely lifelike sculptures.

All about Labeling art

Imagine if colors did not have names. How would you describe a sunset, or a rainbow? In the same way, labeling different kinds of art helps us to understand and compare them.

Find it!
Six tiny cubist paintings are on these pages. Find them!

Not all countries label art in the same way. Here are some names for various types of art made in Europe and America.

① Looking back
◊ RENAISSANCE

During the 1300's, 1400's, and 1500's, there was a great interest in the art of ancient Rome and Greece. Artists painted and carved subjects based on old statues and buildings. They also learned how to make their work more lifelike.

This picture is called *The Skiff*. It was painted around 1879 by the French impressionist artist Pierre Auguste Renoir (1841-1919).

② The great outdoors
◊ IMPRESSIONISM

This style began in France during the late 1800's. Artists painted pictures of everyday scenes and often worked outdoors to try to capture the changing effects of the light. Paintings sometimes looked hurried and unplanned.

③ A new way of seeing
◇ CUBISM

During the early 1900's, artists began to look at objects in a fresh way. They broke down a subject into simple shapes and often included different views of a subject in the same painting. These artists were called cubists.

 show me

This cubist painting was made in 1914 by the Spanish artist Pablo Picasso (1881-1973). Can you spot parts of a musical instrument and a playing card?

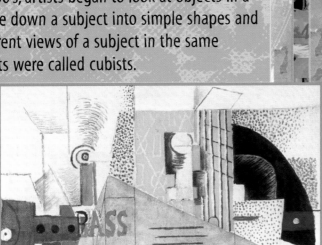

 **follow me**

Art shows us how the world has changed. Follow me to page 22.

④ Using dreams
◇ SURREALISM

This style began in Paris in the 1920's. Artists painted everyday objects and scenes in unusual and often strange ways. Many created dreamlike images.

 tricky test time

Match the works of art to their labels.

A   B

C   D

◇ SURREALIST ◇ CUBIST ◇ POP ◇ IMPRESSIONIST

⑤ Borrowing ideas
◇ POP ART

This style was popular during the 1950's and 1960's. Many pop artists got their ideas from magazines, comic strips, advertisements, and even labels on cans of food!

The American pop artist Andy Warhol (1928-1987) was inspired by the Campbell's soup label to create this work of art, made in 1962.

In other parts of the world...

IN AUSTRALIA
"X-ray painting" is a traditional form of art of the Australian Aborigines. This art, pictured below, shows people, animals, and fish from both the outside and the inside at the same time.

IN JAPAN
From the 1500's to the 1800's, many Japanese artists painted in a style that used simple, strong lines and bold, flat colors. Common subjects included animals, flowers, and landscapes.

 follow me

Follow me to page 21 to see another example of Japanese art.

15

For many artists, making art is a

Way of life

Some artists make art because they enjoy it, others have something to say. Being an artist can become the most important thing in a person's life.

Can anyone be an artist?

When you are young, you enjoy looking around you and making pictures of what you see. You need no training – you do it naturally. If you want to, you can keep on doing this for the rest of your life. Anyone can be an artist!

Find it!

There are three tiny islands on these pages with an artist painting on each. Find them!

Being taught

In the 1500's, special art schools, called academies, were set up in Italy. Students were taught that they should follow certain rules if they wanted to make good art. Today, artists are still taught basic rules, but are also encouraged to use their own ideas.

No teachers!

Some artists have never been shown how to paint or sculpt. They may know little about the history of art. They make art because they want to and feel able to do so.

follow me

Artists have tried many new ways of making art. Follow me to page 20.

On the move

Artists often move around to look for new ideas. In 1891, the French painter Paul Gauguin (1848-1903) went to live on an island in the South Pacific Ocean. He wanted to escape from Europe so that he could find his own style of painting.

tricky test time

To find out where Gauguin made his home, just pick an island and follow the twisty route. The correct answer will lead you to Gauguin himself!

FIJI
TAHITI
HAWAII
GUAM
TONGA

The French artist Henri Rousseau (1844-1910) devoted his life to art. He gave up his job in Paris and taught himself to paint. He is called a primitive or naive artist because he had no training. He made this painting, called *Tropical Storm with a Tiger (Surprise)*, in 1891.

Called to be an artist

The Dutchman Vincent van Gogh (1853-1890) turned to painting during the last 10 years of his life. He felt that it was the only thing he could do. Although most of Van Gogh's work is brightly colored and full of life, he was an unhappy man.

show me

Van Gogh painted *The Church at Auvers-sur-Oise* in 1890. He used thick paint and his brushstrokes seem to move on the canvas. Experiment with making swirling brushstrokes with different types of paint and brushes.

Making money

Galleries are buildings in which artists show their work. Part of the money made from any work that is sold is given to the owners of the galleries. The rest of the money is kept by the artists. Many artists work so that they can make money. Some make no money at all!

tricky test time

Find the answers to these problems to discover some facts about money and art.

1 Vincent van Gogh painted *Portrait of Dr Gachet* in 1890. It sold in 1990 for about:
$24 million + $24 million + $30.5 million = ?
2 Pablo Picasso's entire collection of work is worth about:
$160 million + $400 million + $240 million = ?

follow me

Follow me to page 21 to see other examples of landscapes.

Making art about
People

Painters, sculptors, and photographers often make people the subjects of their work. They record the lives of important and famous people, of those around them, and of themselves.

Thousands of years ago...

The Olmec people lived in Mexico at least 2,000 years ago. They carved giant stone sculptures of human heads.

Around 5,000 years ago, in ancient Egypt, people were often drawn flat. The eye, shoulders, and body faced the front, but the head, legs, arms, and feet were shown from the side.

Find it!
There are 10 tiny heads on these pages. Find them!

LOOKING INSIDE PEOPLE
Around 1500, Leonardo da Vinci cut open dead bodies to help him to understand how muscles and bones worked. He was one of the first people to accurately draw the inside and outside of a human body.

LEARNING FROM THE LIVING
Artists learn more about the human body by drawing nude models. Such pictures are called life drawings. These and other portraits are completed in sittings — times when subjects sit or pose before artists.

show me

Draw a portrait of someone you know. Before you start, answer these questions:

◊ How big will it be?
◊ What materials will you use?
◊ Will the portrait be realistic or not?
◊ How much of your subject will you show?
◊ Should the subject smile or be serious?
◊ Will there be anything else in the picture?

Not realistic

Henry Moore (1898-1986) was an English sculptor. He divided the body into simple shapes and made large sculptures in stone, wood, and bronze. His figures are solid, with smooth, curved lines.

This bronze sculpture was made in 1951. It is called *Reclining Figure: Festival* and shows a woman lying down.

Super realistic

The American sculptor Duane Hanson (1925-1996) made life-sized models of people doing everyday things. His sculptures are extremely realistic and have real hair and clothes.

This sculpture is called *Caddie*. It was made in 1970.

 follow me

Art records the way people's lives change over the years. Follow me to page 22.

---

 tricky test time

Make your own Henry Moore-style sculpture. Which four pieces do you need to use to make this figure?

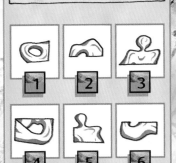

YOU AND YOUR FAMILY

In the past, rich people paid artists a lot of money to paint their portraits. Today, many people take photographs or make video recordings of themselves and their families. This is faster and less expensive!

ART ABOUT YOU

When artists make themselves the subjects of their art, their works are called self-portraits. The Dutch artist Rembrandt (1606-1669) made about one hundred self-portraits. This is one he painted in 1669 when he was 63 years old.

show me

On a sunny day, stand near a wall so that you cast a shadow on it. Ask a friend to trace around the shadow on a sheet of paper. Color it black to make your very own shadow portrait!

19

Let's look at
Art and nature

Many artists make art about nature and the world around them. Some use natural materials in their work.

Find it!
There are two apples and two white flowers on these pages. Can you spot them?

Making choices

Artists may choose to make art about animals or plants. They may show a view of the land, called a landscape, or of the sea, called a seascape. They may paint a small area or a vast expanse.

show me

Here is one way of choosing an area to draw. Make two pieces of cardboard like this. Hold them so that they form a rectangle. Slide the pieces around until they frame a view you like.

Using nature itself

1 WALKING AND COLLECTING
Since the 1960's, the English artist Richard Long has made art by going on walks and recording what happens to him and what he sees. He also collects natural materials, such as stones, and uses them to make sculptures.

2 ROCKY SPIRAL
In 1970, the American artist Robert Smithson (1938-1973) made *Spiral Jetty*. He used rocks to build a curved path in the Great Salt Lake in Utah.

3 SAYING IT WITH FLOWERS
The Scottish artist Anya Gallaccio uses real flowers in her work. In 1995, she made giant chains of flowers and hung them from the roof of a gallery.

Two different ways of seeing nature

① Turner

Joseph Turner (1775-1851) was an English painter of landscapes and seascapes. He was interested in the atmosphere, or mood, of a place. His work is full of shimmering mists, dazzling light, and color.

This painting, made around 1844, is called *Rain, Steam and Speed, the Great Western Railway.* Can you see the train and the bridge?

② Hokusai

The Japanese artist Katsushika Hokusai (1760-1849) is famous for his landscape prints (pictures printed from blocks of wood). He used bold lines and often only the colors blue, brown, and green.

 follow me

Both of these images look modern, yet they were made more than 150 years ago. What will art be like in the future? Follow me to page 23.

This print, called *Mount Fuji on a Clear Day,* was made around 1825.

TRICKS OF THE TRADE

Artists can show distances and make their pictures look real, even on flat surfaces. They use rules of perspective. Distant objects are drawn smaller than nearer ones and are placed closer together.

 show me

Look at the perspective lines drawn over this picture. Can you see how the lines all lead to the same spot? This gives the appearance of depth.

 tricky test time

In this landscape, the English artist William Hogarth (1697-1764) has broken the rules of perspective on purpose. Can you spot five things that are wrong with this picture?

Still life

A still life is a painting or drawing of a group of objects arranged together. Still lifes often show natural objects, such as flowers and fruit. The French painter Paul Cézanne (1839-1906) painted more than 200 still lifes. Many of them were of apples.

Art can Tell tales

Art can give us clues about the past. It shows us how people dressed, what they believed in, and what their interests were. Art also records the present – and the future!

Find it!

There are five tiny globes on these pages. Can you spot them?

① History lessons

In 1937, German planes bombed a Spanish town called Guernica. Hundreds of people were killed or injured. The artist Pablo Picasso was horrified by the event. He made a huge painting to show the pain and suffering of the people of Guernica.

② Family tree

Some North American Indian tribes built tall totem poles outside their homes. The poles were carved with symbols, faces, and animals to record the histories of the families living there.

③ Everyday life

From the 1600's to the 1800's, many Japanese artists made prints and paintings called ukiyo-e. They showed scenes from everyday life. They recorded what people at the time looked like, what they wore, and how they entertained themselves.

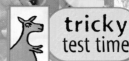
④ Changing times

Art can show us how people's appearances and lifestyles have changed over time.

show me

Both of these paintings have people as their subjects, but can you spot the differences between them? For example, one room is colorful, and the other is gloomy. What about the clothes and the furniture, or the way in which the people are sitting or standing? What do the two pictures have in common?

This family was painted in 1742 by the German artist Marcus Tuscher (1705-1751).

Some art is made to intrigue and entertain people. This painting is called *The Vegetable Gardener*. It was painted in 1570 by the Italian artist Giuseppe Arcimboldo (1527-1593).

The subject is a bowl of food, but can you see what else this picture shows?

What next?

These two people were painted in 1970 by the English artist David Hockney.

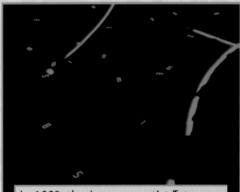

In 1993, the Japanese artist Tatsuo Miyajima presented a work called *Running Time*. It was made up of hundreds of small screens that flashed red, digital numbers in a darkened room. The screens moved across the floor on tiny wheels.

CHANGING TIMES BRING NEW IDEAS

When European museums first exhibited African art, many Western artists were amazed because it was very different from anything they had seen before. Some were so inspired that they began to paint and sculpt in similar ways.

The art of the future will depend on the machines and materials available to artists, their imagination and skill, and the stories they want to tell the world. Anything could happen!

So that's the end of your journey. Now you know (almost) everything about making art!

tricky test time

THE ANSWERS P4: C is not art – it is a brick wall. P7: Islam = writing from Islam's holy book, the Koran; Hinduism = a Hindu god called Shiva; Shintoism = a Shinto goddess called Amaterasu; Christianity = the Virgin Mary and Jesus Christ. P8: 2-yellow; trees; houses; clouds and mountains. P9: Mona Lisa; 1503. P10: F – cochineal is made from the dried bodies of Mexican ants; T; F – burnt sienna is made from burned earth; T. P13: B, C, D, E, and F. P15: A = impressionist; B = pop; C = surrealist; D = cubist. P17: (top) Tahiti; (bottom) 1 = $78.5 million; 2 = $800 million. P19: 2, 3, 4, and 6. P21: the bird in the tree is too big; the distant sheep should be getting smaller; the tiles the man is standing on are upright; the sign dips behind the trees; the woman could not reach the man's pipe (these are just five impossibilities, but there are many more). P23: turn the picture upside down to reveal the vegetable gardener himself!